'Happiness is when what you think, what you say, and what you do are in harmony.'

Mahatma Gandhi

THE
HAPPINESS
YEAR

HOW TO FIND JOY
IN EVERY SEASON

TARA WARD

Illustrated by
Anastasia Stefurak

Hardie Grant

QUADRILLE

For my dear Sis and Bro and for all the wonderful online get-togethers we have had over the past two years, often discussing our thoughts and experiences of the different seasons, each of us appreciating them in different ways. Both of you have taught me a great deal and I love you.

CONTENTS

WELCOME

Welcome to *The Happiness Year*: this is a book that will encourage you to discover different kinds of happiness at profound levels throughout the year, focusing on what matters most to you during each season.

Often your mood and wellbeing are affected by the changing weather, either consciously or unconsciously. Seasons tend to be associated with certain behaviours: spring with new awakenings; summer with sociable relaxation; autumn with harvesting and gathering in; winter with hibernating. So, how often do you tend to fall into patterns of behaviour through the year, based on a belief of how you should be and what you ought to feel? What would happen if you let go of some of those beliefs?

Individuals are complex with varying needs. In this book, alongside traditional attitudes, you will be encouraged to explore different ways of discovering happiness through each season, based on what appeals to you personally. Some suggestions are light-hearted and fun, some go into a deeper level of consciousness. You can choose what you want to try but collectively they will help you in a holistic way – physically, mentally, emotionally and spiritually – so that your happiness will come from deep inside you and will help to nurture your everyday life, making it easier and more enjoyable.

WHAT IS HAPPINESS?

It is important to define happiness in some way before you read any further because the intention of this book is not for you to try to live in a state of constant, heightened pleasure – which would be unrealistic and tiring. It is enlightening when you read different definitions for happiness because they offer some lovely words: content, successful, safe, relaxed, lucky, worthwhile, meaningful, satisfied. Aren't they life-affirming? Which words are you drawn to most? Which of these words are lacking most in your life right now?

Personal happiness can take a myriad of different forms, from an exhilarating buzz that makes your heart speed up, through to a calm, inner stillness that leaves you feeling a deep sense of peace, and everything in between. This book will help you access more of what happiness means for you as an individual, without feeling pressure to conform in any way. You may find it means different things to you in each season. How uplifting to think of spreading happiness throughout every year in a variety of ways, according to how you would like to experience it.

WHY IS HAPPINESS IMPORTANT?

Often the word 'happiness' is referred to in a vague way, but did you know that positive chemicals are released in your body when you're happy? This is something specific and tangible that happens. There are four chemicals, often put into the acronym 'DOSE'. They will be referred to during this book so here is a brief summary of what they are and how they differ:

1. Dopamine: is a chemical messenger that transmits between your nerve cells, sending signals to your brain. You know that quick rush you get when something nice happens? That is dopamine in action.

2. Oxytocin: is a hormone released by the pituitary gland and is connected with social bonding. When you have that warm, fuzzy feeling after physical contact or close emotional connection, oxytocin is being released.

3. Serotonin: is a key hormone that stabilizes your mood and impacts your whole body, affecting your nerve cells and brain function. It can help regulate sleep and digestion, as well as your mood. Feeling proud of your accomplishments can raise your serotonin levels.

4. Endorphins: are a group of peptides produced by your pituitary gland and nervous system that affect the opiate receptors in your brain. Often called the 'feel-good' chemical, this relates to the feelings you get after strenuous physical exercise or even laughing until your stomach hurts. Endorphins can reduce pain signals and boost pleasure.

It is important to activate all of these chemicals because holistic happiness comes from a combination of them. You may know already from reading about DOSE that you tend to experience some but not all of these responses. The exercises in this book are designed to encourage all of these happiness chemicals, so have fun exploring them.

HOW TO ENJOY THIS BOOK

The book is divided into the four seasons, but it doesn't matter which season you read first: perhaps it is the one you like the most, a season you find challenging or whichever time of year you are in as you read this book. Enjoy exploring in any order you wish.

Read through all the seasons because many exercises can be adapted easily for the different times of the year. If you find an exercise you like in spring, for example, then you could tweak it slightly to use in winter.

If you come across an exercise that is difficult for you to do for whatever reason, be kind to yourself and either modify it or move on to another one. Be mindful of your own health and capabilities and know that there is no pressure for you to complete everything.

What matters most is that you enjoy the journey of uncovering for yourself what happiness means to you throughout the year, so that you can improve your quality of life and raise your happiness levels during each season.

SPRING

'Can words describe the fragrance
of the very breath of spring?'

Neltje Blanchan

Feeling happy isn't always a natural response but you can choose to be happy.

Often considered the time of reawakening, nature in the spring shows us signs of new life: snowdrops and crocuses push their way through the still-cold earth and leaves uncurl slowly on the trees. The greys and browns of winter mutate into countless shades of green, punctuated by bright splashes of colour. Swathes of yellow daffodils herald the warm sunshine to come.

Perhaps you find this uplifting and welcoming and, if you do, that is wonderful. You can make the most of that energy during this section and build on your happiness within it. It is okay if you feel differently too. You will find a host of exercises ahead to help you connect with the energies of spring in a way that is meaningful for you.

You might find it helpful to have an intention of what you believe would make you happy as you start this spring section because it could focus your thoughts. If there is something you would like to accomplish, notice how the exercises make you feel in relation to this. You may be inspired. It is fine if you don't have any intentions at this stage and simply want to enjoy a free flow of exploration. There is time at the end of each section to reflect and to create or finalize intentions, if you wish.

CONNECTION

CONNECTING WITH THE ENERGIES OF SPRING

Let's start straight away with a simple exercise and explore what comes up for you in relation to spring. Take a piece of A4 paper and place it in front of you. Write the word SPRING in large letters at the very bottom of the sheet. Now close your eyes and take three comfortable breaths in and out. If you can, breathe in through your nose and out through your mouth. Now open your eyes and look down at the word SPRING on your paper. What immediately comes to mind? Write it down. You can have as many different responses as you like. There are no right or wrong, good or bad answers – just what is true for you. When you feel you have run out of ideas, close your eyes, focus on three more breaths in and out, then repeat the process. Do this several times, if you wish, and take your time. Notice if images come into your mind and describe those, too.

When you are ready, sit back and study what you have written. What jumps out at you the most? Circle or highlight it, if you like. Circle more than one thing if several things seem important. Are there any surprises? What is your overriding emotion as you look at your words? Write that emotion at the top of your paper. It's fine if there is more than one emotion.

Look through any words that relate to making you feel happy and make a separate list of those. As you go through the following exercises, keep referring to this list and notice when those positive words are triggered for you.

MAKE CONNECTIONS WITH PEOPLE

Choose to connect with new people or reconnect with people you may have lost touch with. Sometimes winter can be a time when you withdraw, so spring is a good opportunity to rekindle communication. Be creative with this and perhaps suggest something different from just meeting for a walk or a drink. Could you throw a ball around, go swimming or attend an evening class together? Simply arranging to speak or meet with someone you enjoy being with will top up your oxytocin levels. It could make someone else's day to hear from you and then you are increasing their dopamine levels, which in turn can affect yours. Fun activities that allow you to connect with others can have a deep effect on your happiness. When you combine these activities with a meeting that creates a lot of laughter and smiles, your endorphins are replenished as well.

BODY

EMERGING NEW LIFE

Now let's try something physical to see what is released for you. You can do as much or as little movement as you wish, depending upon your situation. If your ability to move is minimal, please don't worry as it is the intention behind the exercise that creates the experience, so you can imagine this happening rather than actually doing it and it works just as well.

Start by curling yourself physically into the smallest shape that you can without it being uncomfortable. Take your time, do it carefully and gently, and slowly pull in each of your limbs. When you occupy the least possible space, close your eyes and take a moment to notice what you are thinking and feeling. Now, equally slowly, start to unfold yourself, keeping your eyes closed if you can, to help focus on what the experience is like. Stretch out each part of your body in an unhurried, deliberate way. Really enjoy unwinding and elongating every part of you and try to concentrate on the sensation in each area of your body as you do so. Relax and wallow in the experience. When you feel you have stretched yourself out as much as possible, still keeping your eyes closed, try to relax and open up even further. Are your fingertips fully extended? Are your toes spread wide? Finally, open your eyes and ask yourself what your dominant emotions are now. Give your whole body a gentle shake.

If your strongest emotions after these last two exercises are uplifting, that is lovely but it's okay if you find it difficult on some levels, too. Finding happiness doesn't mean we have to try to block out sadness. If you have lost a loved one, seeing new life around you can be an emotional reminder that they are no longer here to enjoy it with you. You might think you ought to feel invigorated and full of new ideas as spring comes. What are you going to accomplish through this year? Perhaps you don't know and that pressure creates some stress. Perhaps the physical exercise made you feel a little vulnerable, rather than alive and renewed.

As you contemplate this season, whatever is happening for you is relevant and meaningful and you are going to find different ways to explore it and find happiness – or perhaps greater happiness – as we go through this section.

TOUCH

A TOUCH OF SELF-COMPASSION

Having explored some of your emotions about spring, take a moment for some self-care.

Place your hand gently over your heart and pat or rub it very gently. Then, if you feel comfortable, wrap your arms around yourself and enjoy a self-hug. Remember the oxytocin mentioned previously, which is one of the DOSE feel-good chemicals your body produces? If you don't have someone to hug, hugging yourself can release oxytocin too. Touch, including self-touch, can be healing and lead to a feeling of gentle comfort.

It doesn't have to be a self-hug if that feels uncomfortable to you. You can wash your body slowly in the shower or bath and then dry yourself carefully and mindfully. You can cut and file your nails or trim your hair. Anything you can do thoughtfully and kindly for yourself through touch can increase feelings of self-compassion and appreciation.

WONDER

HONEYBEE HAPPINESS – WHAT MAKES YOU AMAZING?

Feeling full of wonder at nature and its incredible capabilities, especially in relation to each season, is a great way to increase happiness levels throughout the year. In this exercise, we are going to focus on the wonderful honeybee.

Bees are amazing creatures. You might think of them just as honey-producers but what they go through to do this is inspirational. They fly at up to 25 miles (40km) per hour and beat their wings 200 times per second. They have 170 odour receptors and perform an elaborate 'waggle dance' in a figure of eight when they return to their hive to show others the direction of the best food source.

In the spring, their dominant activity is to swarm together and go off to form new hives. Yet this intense activity is also when the bees are at their most relaxed and friendly.

Using just these few facts about bees as a guide, think about yourself:

• What is amazing about you?

• What might you take for granted about yourself that is wonderful?

Write it down: 'I am amazing because ...' and list everything you can think of. Take your time. It can be anything from the wonders of the human body you inhabit through to your personal talents and abilities. Notice how you feel as you acknowledge yourself. This helps to raise serotonin levels in your body.

ACHIEVING YOUR SPRING PURPOSE

Now think of the spring action of the bees. They have a clear purpose and are taking action to realize that objective. Ask yourself what you would like your purpose to be this spring; it can be as modest or as expansive a goal as you like. As you think of it, ask yourself how realistic it is and how you might accomplish it. If you feel a rush of excitement or enthusiasm as you do this, let that flow through you and enjoy it. Look back over what makes you amazing and see how that links to your intention. How will those qualities help you? Who do you need to communicate with to make this succeed? Write down what needs to happen for your inspiration to take root firmly and to blossom. Add a timeline if you can.

UNDERSTANDING

SPRING INTO SEASONAL HAPPINESS

There are so many other amazing facts about the natural world in spring that you might want to consider and use as a springboard for your own happiness. Think about how you could emulate nature in your own actions.

• Birds are more vocal as they try to attract mates and discourage rivals.

• Studies indicate that male sperm count is highest at this time of year.

• Egypt's Great Sphinx was built so that it points exactly towards the rising sun at the moment of the spring equinox.

• Tornadoes occur most frequently.

• Some people believe in the phenomenon 'spring fever', which refers to feeling restless and daydreaming more than usual.

How do these facts alter your perceptions of spring? What facts help you to understand the happy elements of your own life?

MOVEMENT

COLD WATER REFRESH

Physical activity awakens endorphins, and as you have done a lot of mind work thus far in this section, it is a good time for this. Please do as much as you can, depending on your mobility. Everything can be adapted according to your own situation.

This is a simple and quick task. Splash cold water over as much of you as you can. If you have limited movement, putting your wrists under cold running water or wrapping a few ice cubes in a cloth and placing it against the back of your neck can be very effective. A cool shower or bath would be great, even if it's very brief. The moment of joy comes not from the action itself, which, for a brief moment, may make you shiver and feel uncomfortable, but from the sensations afterwards as endorphins rush through your body. Remember it can be as mild or intense as you want as everyone has different tolerance thresholds. It is not a competition.

QUICK MOVEMENT UPLIFT

Choose a rapid, repetitive movement that you can do for up to five minutes, without it causing you physical stress. It could be marching quickly or running on the spot. You might want to lift and lower your arms quickly: up, out to the side and up again. Do it for five minutes if possible but, if not, do what you can, especially if you feel your heart rate increasing dramatically. Be mindful of your own limits. Take a moment when you finish to focus on how your body feels afterwards and the emotions you have as a result.

THE DARK SECRET OF CHOCOLATE

If physical mobility is difficult for you, apart from imagining the movements, there are other ways to increase your endorphins and these will be discovered as you read through all the seasons, although here is a fun one: eat a piece of dark chocolate. Yes, it's true. A piece of dark chocolate can help raise endorphins. How great is that? Note, one piece is recommended (well, all right, perhaps two), but not a large quantity at once.

SCENT

THE NATURAL FRAGRANCE OF SPRING

Finding happiness through your olfactory system can be a wonderful discovery, especially if you haven't explored it fully before. You can do it in several ways: one is through flowers and their scents. The best-known spring flowers are probably: crocus, daffodil, tulip, iris, bluebell and lily of the valley. Each one has a very different scent and you can find out which makes you feel the most uplifted by experimenting. A flower shop or stall is a great starting point if you don't have a garden, park or woods nearby.

Taking a walk amongst nature and focusing on the smells can be wonderful, too. If you close your eyes and cover your ears, it may enhance your ability to pick up the fragrances. Breathe deeply and try to separate all the smells that you can. Take your time. The more you focus, the more you are likely to realize you don't know what some of them are. Open your eyes and explore. Can you determine where some are coming from? What do you like the most? What makes you smile as you breathe it in? What makes you happy?

EXPLORING ESSENTIAL OILS

There are so many essential oils on offer and some might seem more suited to one particular season. For spring, delightfully astringent grapefruit, lemon or peppermint are recommended as they are good for awakening energy; more soothing choices are geranium, chamomile and bergamot. A session where you smell different essential oils is a fun way to connect with the joy of scent.

NURTURE

ENJOYING SEASONAL FLAVOURS

Increasing happiness in your life also depends upon nurturing different aspects of yourself. What you eat affects how you feel on so many different levels. Spring heralds renewal and the wonders of early crops that are available to enjoy. Have you ever dug up new potatoes or watched strawberries ripen and then picked them to eat immediately? Asparagus is another spring joy, as well as spinach, lettuce and peas. If you don't grow fruit or vegetables, start learning about the times of the year that different fresh fruit and vegetables become available and look out for them in the shops. Really appreciate how much better seasonal produce tastes and relish eating healthy food that makes you feel good as you increase your dopamine levels.

HOW CAN YOU CHERISH YOURSELF?

How could you nurture yourself on an emotional level during the spring? What would you like to focus on that makes you feel good? Think of the aspects of nature that you have read about so far in this section and ask yourself what you need to feel good about the year ahead of you. If you wish, put your hand gently over your heart or your navel area, and think about what the word 'nurture' means to you at this time. When you connect with yourself deeply, the answers that can come to you are amazing.

FINDING YOUR WAY TO RELAX

Lastly, think back to our wonderful honeybees and consider how the bees' actions, although intense, are also relaxed. How can you maintain the equilibrium between self-nurture and activity as you accomplish your goals? What would help you to relax and enjoy this process? Write down some ideas for yourself.

CREATIVITY

GROW YOUR OWN PLANTS FROM SEED

Choosing a creative activity to do during a season, especially one you can really enjoy, gives you a purpose and can also be a lot of fun. You might have your own ideas of what you'd like to do but if you are interested in gardening, try this.

Plant a seed from something you have eaten. It can be anything: apple, avocado, pepper, melon. Why not try several different seeds at once and see which ones germinate? The joy from watching something grow that you have planted can be so satisfying.

As you enjoy this activity, ask yourself what elements of yourself you would like to grow and build upon that would make you feel happier. Make a note of what you decide and put it somewhere you can see it frequently, to remind you. You might want to keep it next to your pot of seedlings.

BREATHING

INHALING THE JOY OF SPRING AIR

Let's look at a simple exercise that gets rid of stale energy in your body, ready to welcome in the new vibrations of spring. It would be good if you could do this in a place with as much fresh air as possible.

You can stand with your weight on both feet or sit upright in a comfortable chair. Take in a deep, comfortable breath and then consciously push it out slowly with the intent of emptying your lungs completely. Focus fully on this sensation. Sometimes saying 'haaaaaa' several times as you do this can help the process, but remember not to breathe in as you vocalize your out-breath. When you think you have no more air to expel, push a little harder and you will be surprised that there is still more to let go. When you are sure there is nothing more to release, enjoy the rush of fresh air as you take in a breath (try not to gulp in the air but let it come into you slowly), then repeat.

With the release of breath, you can also imagine letting go of any stresses or upset you have inside. Then, as you breathe in, imagine a pure white light of joy entering you through the top of your head and, as you breathe out, imagine the white light spreading slowly through every part of your body.

This can make you feel almost heady with pleasure, so make sure you can sit if you need to do so. Doing this in the midst of nature, especially with fresh sea air, adds to the joy.

MEDITATION

HOW TO MEDITATE WITH NATURE

Find somewhere peaceful to sit or lie where you won't be disturbed. Close your eyes and slowly let yourself settle. Take a few comfortable breaths in and out, enjoying the sensation of your body relaxing and your mind releasing any unwanted thoughts.

Now imagine that you are somewhere that is filled with many trees and flowers. It is spring and everything is still in tight bud. It could be somewhere you know or a place you create. Take your time. Notice this place makes you feel peaceful and contented. Slowly walk around it for a few moments, appreciating what is there, and then notice there is somewhere comfortable to sit; you do so. Take a few breaths in and out and, as you relax, you look around and notice the leaves on the trees are opening and all the flowers are beginning to blossom, slowly at first and then more quickly. You watch the scene transform in front of you from green and brown into many shades of beautiful colours. You may realize you are smiling; you feel a release and a lovely sense of wellbeing and pleasure.

As you appreciate the joy around you, decide to ask yourself:

• How do I want to emerge this spring?

• What colour or colours am I?

• How am I blooming?

• How would I like to be in this world, both for myself and for others?

Be aware of your responses and how they make you feel.

Then, when you are ready, slowly withdraw from your scene and let it recede from you. When it is gone, take a moment to focus on your body and notice how heavy and comfortable it feels. Slowly, open your eyes and reorient yourself. Wait a moment before you get up. You may want to make some notes about what happened to you during the meditation.

REFLECTION AND INTENTION

You have come to the end of the exercises for spring, so now is the opportunity for you to reflect on what you have learned about your personal relationship with happiness during this season. It might be helpful for you to write down some specific thoughts on how you intend to enjoy all that spring has to offer.

SET YOURSELF A GOAL

Creating your own intention for each season, and following it through, is a powerful way to feel good about yourself. Research shows that finding a need or purpose and achieving that purpose adds to your happiness in a way that can be measured tangibly by increased levels of the hormones in your body that make you feel good. It is also interesting to note that your happiness doesn't depend on doing a task brilliantly but simply from being better at it than you expected. Therefore, if you set yourself a realistic target, without being too tough on yourself, the pride that comes from succeeding gives you a boost of happiness.

It's important to choose an intention that inspires and excites you. We are all different so what works for one person may not resonate with someone else. You might have had an idea of your aim at the start of this section. Has it changed or has your resolve become firmer? If you are uncertain still, ask yourself the following:

• What would I like to do that inspires me?

• What goal would I look forward to doing that makes me feel happy as I work on it?

• What is realistic that I know I can accomplish?

If, after answering these questions, you remain unclear about your intentions for this season, here are some simple suggestions:

• Find three reasons to smile every day and make a note of them. Put them into practice.

• Discover one new, amazing fact about spring every day and ask yourself what you can learn from it and how it could inspire you personally.

• Every day, write down at least one positive thing you did.

MAKING A PLAN

Once you have chosen your purpose for spring, mark out as clearly as you can how you will accomplish it. Remember to make it realistic. However detailed or simple it may be, ensure that the process is one you will enjoy. Set out ways to keep on track and give yourself clear timeframes. Perhaps factor in 'reward moments' along the way to motivate you. The more specific you can be, the more likely you are to follow it through and enjoy, not just the task itself, but the sensations when you complete it successfully.

KEEPING A JOURNAL

One way to keep track of what will make you feel happy is for you to keep a regular journal. If you can, write down your thoughts, feelings and experiences every day, and try to include at least two positive things each time. Have one positive thing be a specific, nice quality within yourself that you appreciate. It could be something as simple as 'Today I had compassion for myself when I felt down'. You might find it difficult at first to do this, but with practice, these positive acknowledgements become easier to recognize and it is a wonderful way to add to your happiness levels.

Love yourself before you love others. Therein lies happiness.

SPRING AFFIRMATIONS

Affirmations are positive statements that you repeat several times every day so that the repetition strengthens and confirms your ability to make them happen. They need to be framed as current and in the present tense in order for your brain to absorb and respond to them.

'I release unwanted energy and embrace new opportunities.'

'I emerge from my cocoon; I am refreshed.'

'I am looking forward to the year ahead.'

'I am achieving new goals.'

'If you want others to be happy, practise compassion. If you want to be happy, practise self-compassion.'

Dalai Lama

SUMMER

'Rest is not idleness,
and to lie sometimes on the grass on a summer
day listening to the murmur of water
or watching the clouds float across the sky
is hardly a waste of time.'

John Lubbock

Appreciate those who make you happy; they are the green-fingered soul gardeners.

Summer is very much associated with warmth, inducing pleasure and relaxation. Nature offers its abundance of flora for birds and animals, who bustle busily to collect its bounty. A myriad of delicious fruits and vegetables ripen for us to enjoy. We shed layers of clothes, feeling lighter in the process, and many families plan breaks away, looking forward to quality time together. Our serotonin levels rise with more sunlight and warmth and oxytocin chemicals are released when we spend time relaxing with loved ones.

How much of the above applies to you? Perhaps you have different feelings, so allow yourself time to explore in the exercises that follow.

If you are someone who enjoys setting goals and achieving them, you might already have an idea of what you would like to do during summer that makes you feel happy. Make a note of your intentions and then notice the impact of the exercises as you do them. Are they confirming your thoughts or encouraging you to change them? Whether you want to create some goals now or formulate them as you go along, enjoy your exploration. There is an opportunity at the end of this section to reflect.

CONNECTION

UNDERSTANDING YOUR MEANING OF SUMMER

Below is a list of words traditionally associated with summer. Go through each word and ask yourself how it may or may not connect with your personal relation to happiness.

• Warmth

• Relaxation

• Holiday

• Seaside

• Travel

• Swimming

• Socializing

• Barbecues

If many of these induce feelings of happiness, that is lovely. If they don't, for whatever reason, ask yourself firstly what they do mean for you, and then ask yourself what makes you personally feel good about summer. Be honest. What one person finds relaxing, another can find stressful, so it is important to understand yourself without trying to conform. If summer is the busiest time of your work year, for example, naturally it will be different for you. What pressures might you find yourself under and how do you respond to them? Tensions in any season can inhibit the release of the DOSE happiness chemicals.

BODY

TENSE AND RELAX

A wonderful way to understand your body better and appreciate the difference between tension and relaxation is to tense the muscles deliberately, then to release them consciously. This can create endorphins, one of your feel-good chemicals. This exercise is simple but it can be a real happiness booster.

Lie down flat, if you can, stretching out your legs and arms, letting your feet splay outwards and your arms rest a little way from your body. Starting with both of your feet, tense your muscles and scrunch them up as tightly as you can for up to five seconds. Then release them and enjoy the feeling of relaxation as it sweeps through that part of you. Take a deep, comfortable breath. Repeat with your lower legs, upper legs, buttocks, torso, arms and fingers and lastly, your face and neck. If you wish, repeat the whole exercise again, but this time tense for longer, for up to 10 seconds. You can make this exercise more detailed as well. For instance, you could start with just your right foot, then focus on your left foot and so on. Isolate whichever parts of your body feel as though they need the most focus.

Notice how you are feeling afterwards. You may be aware of the blood flowing much more freely through your body and a lovely sense of relaxation that engulfs you. Repeat this exercise whenever you can and try to carry this sensation of letting go through the summer, allowing the warmth of this season to further enhance your sense of wellbeing.

TOUCH

MINDFUL BATHING

Skin and hair can become dry in the summer, especially if you are out and about in the sun. The next time you put lotion on your body, or wash your hair, try doing it mindfully. That means making the whole experience a pleasure for all your senses. Treat yourself to a product that smells pleasing to you. Odour affects our taste buds, so you might enjoy choosing a scent related to food, such as coconut, apple or strawberry. Start off by putting some of the product onto your hands and slowly rubbing them together. Take your time. How does the scent make you feel? What is the liquid like on your skin? Look at the liquid and notice its colour and what that means to you. Now rub it slowly and carefully over your hair or body. Notice whether your hair or skin feels rough or smooth; how do different areas contrast? What areas of your head or body do you enjoy touching most? What sounds are you hearing as you do this, no matter how subtle? Notice areas that make you feel emotional or uncomfortable and ask yourself why. Appreciate aspects of your hair and body you may not have noticed before.

Take as long as you can and then, when you are finished, wipe your hands gently and carefully. Take a moment to ask yourself how your hair or body are feeling now. How different was it to experience this simple task mindfully, rather than hastily or carelessly? Moments of mindfulness, no matter how brief, play an enormous role in happiness. Connecting with yourself through all your senses in this way releases oxytocin, one of our feel-good hormones. If you can fit in a moment of mindful cleansing and nurturing this way, it will help you through all the seasons.

WONDER

WATER IS WONDERFUL

Keeping hydrated is important throughout the year but especially during the heat of the summer; never can still water taste so good as during this time. The heat and dryness might make it feel as though your thoughts and creativity are drying up. Some people say they can't think straight in the heat. Always make sure you drink sufficient water and keep some with you. Such a simple thing as being properly hydrated can make an enormous difference to how good you feel.

FOG DRIP

Nature holds amazing wonders so discovering interesting facts may inspire you, especially if you relate them back to your own life.

Have you heard of fog drip? This is common in coastal areas where rain doesn't fall much, such as California in the USA. Fog drip is a vital part of the ecosystem there. Fog rolls in off the coast during the summer, condenses onto the leaves and pine needles of the trees and then drips onto the ground, providing essential moisture. One night of fog drip is enough to provide 1mm of precipitation without a drop of actual rain falling. Nature can be so clever. You can always tell which area has benefitted from fog drip because the ground below the tree will be more verdant than any other.

As you reflect on this phenomenon and its positive outcome, consider your own wellbeing during the summer months. What effect do arid conditions have on you: mentally, physically, emotionally and spiritually? What sort of fog drip do you need to boost your own health? How might it be created for you?

It could be as basic as keeping better hydrated, or your moisture might need to come from another nurturing source, such as cooling your body temperature with the Cold Water Refresh (page 26) discussed in spring. If you have the opportunity to go swimming – be it in the sea, a lake or river – does that appeal? What else refreshes and hydrates you?

Simply washing your hair and then leaving it to dry naturally can feel refreshing and smell uplifting.

UNDERSTANDING

THE NATURAL WORLD

There are many aspects of the natural world to inspire you. Other fascinating facts to explore about summer include:

• Find out about hummingbird hawk moths that migrate north from southern Europe in summer in variable numbers.

• Discover how you can work out the temperature from the frequency of crickets' chirps.

• Search for online live-stream cameras and watch how bears eat massive quantities of food to prepare for winter hibernation.

• Look up when the most visible annual meteor shower will take place in summer.

• Research the massive volcanic eruption of Mount Tambora in Indonesia in 1815, the devasting effects of which meant 1816 became known as 'the year without a summer'.

Whatever you explore, take time to relate what you find back to yourself and observe how it makes you feel. Notice the facts that uplift and inspire you and make you feel happy.

MOVEMENT

STRETCH INTO THE MORNING

Stretching can be more enjoyable during the summer because the warmer weather helps your muscles to relax and in turn makes them more flexible. A wonderful way to start your day, rather than getting out of bed straight away, is to take a moment to stretch your whole body. The happiest way to do this is languidly and gently, without forcing anything. If physical mobility is difficult for you, remember you can use your thought processes to imagine the movement and that alone will help to relax you.

Lie flat on your back, if you can do so comfortably. Breathe in and then, as you breathe out, gently stretch your arms and fingers towards the ceiling as high as you can. Breathe in and then breathe out as you lower your arms slowly and let them relax by your sides. Repeat three times. Then, keeping your legs flat if you can, point your toes and, on an out-breath, feel your lower torso reaching across to the wall at the foot of your bed. Remember to be gentle, don't force anything. Breathe in and then, as you breathe out, flex your toes as much as you can. Relax. Repeat this three times. Next, sit up slowly, keeping your legs straight out in front of you. Bending from the hips, breathe in and then, on an out-breath, slowly stretch your arms up over your head and then over and along your legs, trying to reach your toes. Breathe in and relax back as you breathe out. Repeat three times.

Simple things such as breathing and stretching can contribute so much to your summer happiness.

SCENT

FINDING SIGNATURE FRAGRANCES

Scent is highly effective in boosting pleasure because it can transport us to significant memories. Here are a few suggestions; feel free to add your own personal choices.

- Clothes drying in the wind.

- Roses or other flowers.

- Freshly mown grass.

- Barbecues.

What happens to your body when you smell these things? What else do you like? Remember to take your time and feel the odour coming in through your nostrils and finding its way down through your whole body. Experiencing it in a mindful way allows you to immerse yourself fully in it, releasing both serotonin and dopamine.

If you find a scent that makes you feel particularly good, how could you recreate it around you on a regular basis? For instance, if the smells of a beach make you feel good but you don't live near to one, how could you bring that happiness to where you are now? It might be that you want to have the sounds of the waves or dolphins playing sometimes, or a candle whose scent reminds you of a beach, or a photo of a beautiful beach that inspires you. Conjuring thoughts of scents can be pleasurable and relaxing.

Certain smells and tastes can have a cooling effect too. Mint, in particular, can revive you during the summer. Sipping fresh mint tea, sprinkling peppermint essence around a hot bedroom, putting a few drops of spearmint essential oil into your shower or bath – all these things can be refreshing.

NURTURE

THE TASTE OF SUMMER

Summer foods can be a joy and a great way to nurture your body. Watermelon is in season in summer and its refreshing taste can be cooling and satisfying for those with a sweet tooth. You might prefer raspberries, peaches or plums. Tomatoes can be easy to grow, along with avocados, courgettes (zucchini) and cucumber. Finding fruits and vegetables in season means your taste buds can appreciate the food even more, so if eating is one of your great pleasures in life, do some research to find out what is available near you that is fresh. Remember to eat food slowly, in small mouthfuls, and chew thoroughly to release the full flavours and to be able to relish the myriad tastes.

There are activities you may know already that you can make fun and different too. Many of us love a summer picnic, but what about giving it a special theme, perhaps based on a country's cuisine or someone's favourite book, sport or show? You could have fun making sandwiches or biscuits in different colours and flavours.

CREATIVITY

EXPLORE YOUR ARTISTIC SIDE

Music and books can feature more during the summer too, as we are able to spend more time relaxing outdoors. What do you like most? You might love to withdraw and enjoy music alone or you might prefer to share it with others. Whilst most of us tend to read alone, what about reading a book out loud with someone else? The sense of social connection through sharing a common experience – discussing your beliefs and enjoying the story – can create happy, intimate moments, raising oxytocin levels.

How about drawing or painting? Research has shown that through art, creativity, social development and self-worth are promoted. This ties in with raising serotonin and oxytocin levels. You don't have to be good at something to enjoy it, so drawing isn't about creating something 'good', it is about enjoying the experience itself. Sitting somewhere warm and peaceful, creating art for pleasure without needing to be proficient, can be a happy, relaxing pastime.

BREATHING

THE COOLING BREATH

The yogic cooling breath called *sitali pranayama* is easy to do and very effective. It is perfect for those times when you feel hot and unfocused.

Fully stick out your tongue and curl the edges up into an 'o'. If you can't do this (and genetically some people can't), then make an 'o' shape with your lips pursed together instead. Now breathe in through your 'o' or curled tongue to a slow count of three or four, close your mouth, hold the breath for one or two seconds, then slowly breathe out through your nose to a count of three or four. Please don't make yourself feel uncomfortable by trying to hold your breath for too long; hold it only for as long as it feels acceptable to you. Repeat this at least three times. Once you have done this a few times, you will discover how refreshing it feels.

MEDITATION

SUMMER SUN MEDITATION

To enjoy this meditation fully, find somewhere beautiful in summer's nature to sit and relax, where you can feel safe and comfortable enough to close your eyes and know you won't be disturbed. If this isn't possible for you, then you can choose to sit in front of an evocative image of summer and reflect on it for a few minutes before you close your eyes.

Find your happy place to rest for a while. Start by relaxing your body, doing a few cooling breaths if you feel hot, or simply focusing on each breath coming in and out of your body. Imagine filling your whole body on each in-breath and feel your body relaxing with each out-breath.

Now open your eyes and look around you (or at your chosen image). What do you see first that makes you feel happy? Take your time. What else? What would you like to touch around you? Notice how it makes you feel when you touch, or imagine touching, that object. Close your eyes. What can you hear (or imagine you can hear)? Enjoy it. What can you smell? Breathe it in fully.

After doing this for a while, ask yourself what you are feeling and thinking that is adding to your happiness. Where in your body are you affected? Take your attention to that area. Keeping your eyes closed, gently place your hand over the area if you can. Try to describe the sensation to yourself and enjoy it.

Now decide you want to relax fully. Do this in whatever way works for you. Sit or lie more comfortably. As you breathe in, feel your muscles start to relax; as you breathe out, feel your body melting into whatever surface you are resting on.

Nothing is an effort; everything feels calm. Enjoy the warmth of your experience; feel it seep into your bones, allowing you to unwind even more.

Stay like this for as long as you can, letting thoughts and images drift in and out, without trying to control them in any way. Relish the release and free flow of energy.

When you are ready, take your focus back to the space you are in now. Open your eyes slowly. Stretch your body, slowly and mindfully. Make sure you feel grounded and balanced before you get up and continue with your day.

REFLECTION AND INTENTION

Now you have tried the exercises, what have you discovered about your levels of happiness in the summer? You may have formulated some intentions by now, but if you haven't, here are further suggestions on how you might enjoy the gifts that summer offers.

RELEASE THAT POSITIVE ENERGY

At a time of year when the weather is often conducive to being outdoors, what would you like to enjoy? You may love certain games during the summer already, such as tennis or soccer, but also ask yourself what game or exercise you have never tried but would like to. Have you enjoyed rockpooling or wild water swimming? What else is available for you to try?

Usually, it is easier to encourage others to come out and play during summer months, so take advantage of this time to enjoy some new, fun activities. Being outside in the sunshine, letting the warmth of the sun seep into you, even for short periods, raises the serotonin levels and makes you feel positive about life.

DON'T PUT YOURSELF UNDER PRESSURE

Whatever tasks or experiences you decide would be right for you, remember to enjoy them! If you have a specific goal, give it a timeframe to encourage you but make sure it is do-able so you don't put undue pressure on yourself. It is better to have several small goals that you can complete and tick off rather than one large one that feels daunting. If the task is large, break it down into chunks that you know you could do, and put timescales against each one. Be kind to yourself if a deadline slips and know you are doing your best. It is fine to revisit timelines and alter them. Working collaboratively with someone else might be another way to have fun along the way and encourage mutual success.

Happiness is a journey, not a destination.

SUMMER AFFIRMATIONS

Repeat these positive statements throughout the day
to remind you that summer happiness is available to
you at any time.

'I relax and have fun every day.'

'I welcome the sun's warmth and let it nurture me.'

'I take pleasure in other people's company.'

'I enjoy playing every day.'

'Summer afternoon – summer afternoon;
to me those have always been the two
most beautiful words in the English language.'

Henry James

AUTUMN

'Delicious autumn!
My very soul is wedded to it,
and if I were a bird I would
fly about the earth
seeking the successive autumns.'

George Eliot

The happiness of
your life depends
on the quality of
your thoughts.

Autumn is a time of glorious colours as the air becomes crisp and warmer clothes are dug out of cupboards. The intense summer sun fades to a weaker glow, which you try to catch with ever-decreasing opportunities. It is a time of harvesting crops, giving thanks for what the summer weather has created and preparing to stock up for winter.

Traditionally seen as a transition season, because it is becoming colder and the daylight hours are shortening, some people can find autumn difficult. Often it is because they are anticipating the winter to come, meaning they are focusing on times ahead, rather than enjoying the here and now. Knowing that, it means that mindfulness is more important than ever during autumn, so that you can enjoy its gifts fully.

Mindfulness has come into focus already in spring and summer, but you are going to start autumn with an awareness exercise to enliven all your senses, so that mindfulness becomes even more pronounced for you.

If you have some ideas about what you enjoy doing during autumn, make a note of them, as that is a positive start. On the other hand, you might find this is a season where you aren't sure what will make you happiest and that is fine too. Using mindfulness, to connect with how you feel as you formulate some intentions, will help you choose what is right for you. You will be encouraged at the end of this section to finalize your thoughts.

CONNECTION

COLOUR YOUR HAPPINESS

More than any other season, autumn brings awareness of colours into sharp focus. So here is an opportunity to deepen your connection to colour in relation to happiness. Look at the autumnal suggestions listed below. What colour appeals most to you? What makes you feel the happiest? What would you like to explore on a more profound level? Take your time.

- Gold

- Yellow

- Brown

- Orange

- Red

- Copper

CONNECT WITH COLOUR ENERGY

When you have chosen a colour, see if you can find an object in that colour. It can be anything: a plate, a hat, a vegetable. If you wish, find your chosen colour online or in a book and keep it in front of you. Perhaps find a piece of art in that colour if you can. Sit comfortably, with your feet flat on the floor, look at your colour for at least 20 seconds and then close your eyes. The colour should still be in your mind's eye.

Now let's play with your colour and see what effect it has on you. Start off by seeing the colour expand in front of you. What is seeing even more of the colour making you think and feel? Now imagine your colour wrapping itself around you...

It can either touch you or stay a distance away from your body. What is that like? Reach out and touch the colour. What does it feel like? Take a piece of the colour and smell it. What is its smell? Hold it up to your ear. Does it have a sound? Imagine putting it into your mouth. What does it taste like? Now see part of the colour becoming a ball and take it. Juggle with it. How does that feel? When you are ready, and if you feel like it, allow some of the colour to travel around your body. Take it to whatever part of your body you feel drawn to. How does it feel inside you? You may choose to let it remain there or to remove it gently.

When you are ready to finish, see the colour fading away in front of you and disappearing slowly into the distance. Notice how that makes you feel. Focus on how heavy your feet feel on the surface below you and how heavy your buttocks are in your chair before you open your eyes again.

How did you find that exercise? You may find colour is much more emotional than you expected. You may have found yourself smiling a great deal during the exercise without noticing it. If you didn't feel much, repeat it with another colour and note the difference.

The more you play with colours, the more you notice them and the more you can enjoy their energy and the positive impact different colours have on your happiness levels. Autumn is a perfect season to enhance your appreciation.

It is fine if you don't feel drawn to any of the colours mentioned above. Feel free to decide what colour you feel more drawn to exploring during autumn. You don't have to conform to the normal shades associated with this time of year; try any colour you like.

BODY

WALKING THROUGH AUTUMN

Autumn is an excellent time to do more walking. It can be muddy in the spring, too hot in the summer and too cold in the winter, but often autumn is perfect! Make sure you have comfortable footwear and clothes that are warm enough but not too thick, and see if you can find somewhere new to walk. If your options are limited, walk in your usual place, but give yourself the challenge of seeing at least three new things on each walk – things that you may not have noticed before. It can be something small: the curve of a tree branch, a tiny plant or even a small insect on the ground. Perhaps make a note of what you observe and what makes you smile the most.

This attention to detail encourages you to be mindful – to be completely absorbed in the moment. When you do this on a walk, it means you aren't dwelling on anything in the past or worrying about something in the future. Those two behaviours can block happiness so it is healthy to let them go as much as possible. Mindful walking takes you fully into the present, able to focus on and enjoy what is happening right now. Combining it with the physical movement of propelling yourself forward means you have a sense of purpose, even if it is subconscious, and this mix means several of your DOSE chemicals are becoming activated at once. It is wonderful what a mindful walk can do for your happiness levels, especially at this time of year.

TOUCH

THE TEXTURE OF AUTUMN

The touch of autumn is very different from that of summer.
With fabrics, the smooth silks and cool cottons are put away
and replaced by thicker sweaters and scarves. Sometimes
their textures can be rougher; how does that make you feel?
Run your hands over your autumn clothes and ask yourself
what you think of them. If they make you feel good, that is
great. If they don't, ask yourself how you could alter them in
some way to improve your experience of touch.

COMPASSIONATE TOUCH

Another mindful joy can be finding a fallen leaf, of a
houseplant or out in nature. Try rubbing a little oil into it,
slowly and gently. Notice how the leaf softens under your
touch; it may become more pliable. The colour may change
too. As you enjoy this process, reflect on yourself. What does
the 'oil' in your life consist of, especially in the autumn? You
are giving the leaf great care and attention; how often do
you give your own body and mind the same care? What
could you do to improve this, knowing compassionate
self-touch could raise your oxytocin levels?

WONDER

NATURAL WONDERS

Monarch butterflies are amazing. Every autumn, millions of them fly approximately 3,000 miles (5,000km) from North America to the forests in Southern Mexico for winter. A new generation migrates each year so they can't learn the route from others; they have to find their way through the sun's position and the earth's magnetic field. On average, they cover 20 to 30 miles (35 to 50km) each day but when necessary, and conditions are favourable, they can do more than 150 miles (250km) per day.

Relate this fact to yourself and think about your own journey in life. How far have you come, metaphorically as well as literally? How often have you had to navigate yourself without help and support from others? How amazing you are. What have you accomplished in your journey that makes you feel proud? When have you had to move quickly? When have you been forced to slow down or chosen to be more leisurely? What has that helped you to learn in life?

You are as special as those monarch butterflies; really take the time to acknowledge yourself and what you have done in your life. If you struggle with this, start a list and add to it whenever you can think of something. It can be a big or small action that made a difference in your life or someone else's. Notice how you feel as you acknowledge yourself. You will be topping up your serotonin levels.

UNDERSTANDING

EXTEND YOUR KNOWLEDGE

Other inspiring autumn nature facts you could look up include the following, but you can take your exploration of the natural world wherever you wish.

• The Arctic tern flies 44,000 miles (71,000km) on its round trip between Greenland and the Antarctic.

• Before c.1500, the autumn season was called simply 'harvest' with the bright harvest moon being essential for farmers to be able to see to harvest their late-year crops.

• The autumn equinox is one of two days a year when the sun is perfectly in line with the earth's celestial equator, giving us exactly 12 hours of light and 12 hours of darkness.

• Many countries never experience autumn at all, such as Greenland and the Antarctic in the North and South Poles, and any countries near the equator including Brazil, Malaysia, Singapore, Indonesia, Philippines and Kenya.

Notice what facts you are drawn to and ask yourself why. How do they relate to you? What positive emotions do they create in you? Research other interesting information about this season.

MOVEMENT

RUNNING THROUGH THE LEAVES

This is such a simple joy, but it seems adults, children and animals alike take great pleasure in it: walk, run or skip through a pile of crisp autumn leaves. Choose a really thick pile if possible, kicking up your legs as high as you can. Bend down and pick up a big armful and scatter them into the wind. Notice what this child-like joy feels like and allow yourself to be immersed in it. Do a dance with the leaves if you want.

Where are you feeling the happiness in your body? Really notice the different muscles you are using and how they feel when you move with a sense of fun and pleasure, without any intention other than enjoying yourself. How often do you choose to move your body in this free-flowing way?

The sound of the dry crunch, the earthy smell of leaves, the myriad of autumnal colours around you: there are so many senses involved in this small action. Use them all if you can, making this delightful movement as mindful as possible.

SCENT

EXPLORE THE SCENTS OF AUTUMN

One of the most common autumnal scents is pumpkin, whether it is the aroma you get from carving the flesh of a fresh one or eating pumpkin pie or soup. How do you respond to this scent? What does it make you feel? How different is it for you touching and carving the flesh as opposed to consuming it? Which do you prefer and why?

If you are drawn to essential oils, cinnamon, bergamot and ginger are popular at this time of year. Remember you can enjoy these scents in different ways. As the nights draw in, what about treating yourself to a candle scented with something that makes you feel good?

If you have the opportunity to light a fire, whether indoors or outdoors, or can attend a bonfire, how does that pungent aroma make you feel? What associations do you have with enjoying fires that might make you feel good?

NURTURE

ENJOYING THE PRESENT MOMENT

Sometimes, attitudes in autumn can be stuck in a sense of knowing what is to come, feeling the year creeping towards its conclusion and a sense of the colder times that are in store. If this is true for you, then nurturing yourself is especially important. There are so many small ways you can do this. Look at the list below and see what you might be drawn to.

• Enjoy a favourite drink, slowly and mindfully. Make it with care and attention to detail, appreciate its aroma and let the liquid linger for a while in your mouth before swallowing. Savour its after-taste as well.

• Set aside an amount of time just for you (even a short break can be beneficial).

• Switch off technology and entertainment systems. Instead, relax and go within. Then remind yourself of how proud you are of yourself.

• Buy a small treat for yourself and don't feel guilty: enjoy it.

• Tell someone you are close to how much you appreciate them and what they mean to you. Be specific in your praise.

• When appropriate, say 'no' to things you don't need or want to do.

CREATIVITY

CHALLENGE YOUR TASTE BUDS

Here is a fun suggestion: did you read earlier that eating small quantities of dark chocolate can raise endorphins? To enjoy this – or at least experience it – in a completely different way, why not try dark chocolate that is flavoured with something unusual? There are a lot available on the market now. For example, you can find lavender, wasabi, green tea and marmite/vegemite, to name but a few. There are even more unusual options such as pizza, soy sauce, potato chips and shiitake mushroom. Waking up your taste buds in a new way can be exhilarating, and if you choose to enjoy the tasting with others whose company you love (how about a chocolate tasting gathering or blind-folded competition of 'guess the flavour'?) you can boost your oxytocin levels at the same time.

SEEKING OUT BEAUTY

Autumn is a time where there is so much to appreciate on the ground in nature. What about taking a walk either alone or with someone and seeing who can find the most beautiful fallen leaf, nut or shell? Perhaps you could incorporate what you find into homemade art in some way.

REVISIT YOUR CHILDHOOD

Another joy can be re-discovering a childhood game that you used to love playing. What have you access to that you could have fun with again? One of the benefits of doing this is that it may transport you back to a time when you were more carefree, with few responsibilities. Rekindling those feelings can induce a lovely sensation of relaxation and happiness. Explore some childhood games and see if this is true for you. If you opt for a game such as hopscotch or skipping with a rope, you get the added benefit of some endorphins kicking in, too.

BREATHING

THE BREATH OF POETRY

Did you know reciting poetry slowly can be a wonderful way to breathe deeply? Try reading the quotes opposite out loud. Read them slowly, savouring each word and sentiment. If you can, try to say each one with only one breath. Repeat each one a few times, getting slower each time. Notice how you feel more relaxed as you do this. It may take a while to be able to read the last two with one breath only as they are slightly longer. What sentiment do you like best? Which is the most pleasurable to read?

'Every leaf speaks bliss to me,
fluttering from the autumn tree.'

Emily Brontë

'How beautifully leaves grow old. How full
of light and colour are their last days.'

John Burroughs

'Autumn is the mellower season, and what we
lose in flowers we more than gain in fruits.'

Samuel Butler

'Autumn is the season to find contentment at home
by paying attention to what we already have.'

Unknown

'There is a harmony in autumn, and a lustre in its
sky, which through the summer is not seen or heard,
as if it could not be, as if it had not been.'

Percy Bysshe Shelley

'I cannot endure to waste anything so precious as
autumnal sunshine by staying in the house. So I have
spent almost all the daylight hours in the open air.'

Nathaniel Hawthorne

MEDITATION

TREE MEDITATION

Stand or sit in a comfortable position. It is better to stay upright rather than lying down, if possible. Close your eyes and let yourself settle. Concentrate on each breath coming in and going out of your body. Don't try to change your breath; simply observe it. Make sure the soles of your feet are resting solidly on the surface below you and that your weight is distributed evenly.

Now focus on your spine and how straight it is, starting with the base of your spine and slowly following each vertebra, right up to your neck. Notice if you feel the urge to sit up straighter as you do this.

With your eyes closed, picture a very tall, solid tree. It stands proud and straight, its leaves coloured with shining autumnal gold. What is your first emotion as you look at the tree? What are you thinking? You approach the tree and run your hand along the bark. What does it feel like? What can you smell as you do this? Put your arms around the tree. How does that make you feel? Now turn around and place your back against the trunk. Let the energy of the tree be absorbed into your spine, making you feel strong and solid. Notice how firm your feet feel on the ground, how balanced you feel.

Now ask yourself: what makes me feel happy about this tree? How does that translate to myself? What would I like to do to make myself even stronger and more resilient?

When you are ready, walk away slowly from the tree and let it fade in your mind's eye. Focus on your body again, give yourself a gentle shake and open your eyes when you're ready. Note down your experience if you wish.

REFLECTION AND INTENTION

You have explored a number of ways to connect with the joy of autumn. How are you feeling now? You may have found some of these exercises emotional and hopefully they have helped you to understand what happiness means to you personally during this season. If you are unsure still, explore some further thoughts on the following pages.

MAKING THE MOST OF THE SEASON OF CHANGE

What would you like to accomplish during autumn, making way for winter? Remember that having a goal will help focus you and keep you mindful. If you find the thought of an upcoming winter hard, accomplishing a task will give you a sense of pride and purpose. For instance, would you consider helping in the community in some way, perhaps giving companionship to people who might be alone or in need of support? Bonding with others boosts your dopamine and serotonin levels. Notice how that thought makes you feel.

Here are some other suggestions:

• You could clear out some clothes or items you don't need and donate them to a good cause. Apart from creating some space for yourself, giving to others makes you feel good too.

• Why not make a commitment to enjoy every day as fully as possible, and to find pleasure in all the small joys around you? Use all five of your senses. Make notes of what you have enjoyed at the end of each day.

EMBRACING CHANGE

Your goals in autumn are likely to encompass the acceptance of change and this is not always easy to do. If finding happiness amongst constant change is hard for you, here are some position actions you could take to help you:

• If you start to worry about the future, simply thank your thoughts for being there and tell them that you choose to release those thoughts for now. If you do this as soon as worry creeps in, it will become a habit and you will find it increasingly easy to do.

• Embrace the realization that nothing is permanent. Whatever is happening now will change and whatever is ahead is transitory too. There is great happiness to be found in the ebb and flow of life.

Making notes about your emotions during autumn and noticing the effect of using these suggestions will help to alleviate anxiety, leaving more space for positive thoughts.

WEATHERING THE STORM

Lastly, reminding yourself how resilient you are is a wonderful way to boost confidence levels. There is a second part to the Tree Meditation on page 91, which may help you with this.

Repeat the Tree Meditation (see page 90) but this time, when you leave, retreat to a covered area and sit. As you observe the tree, the wind starts to whip up and heavy rain falls. You see the tree's branches waving but not breaking; you watch the leaves falling to the ground. You notice how strong and solid the tree is and how it can withstand the storm; it bends and moves with the wind when necessary. Relate this to yourself and how you have weathered storms already and will continue to weather any that come in future. How does that make you feel?

Remember that happiness comes, not from a lack of challenges, but in how we respond to them.

AUTUMN AFFIRMATIONS

In many ways, autumn seems to highlight change.
You can increase your happiness levels if you choose
to embrace each moment.

'I am grateful for today.'

'I live in the moment.'

'Colours uplift and inspire me.'

'I am strong and flexible.'

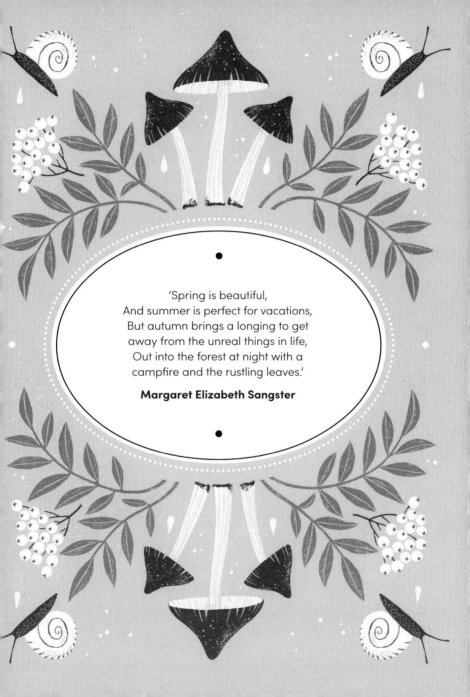

'Spring is beautiful,
And summer is perfect for vacations,
But autumn brings a longing to get
away from the unreal things in life,
Out into the forest at night with a
campfire and the rustling leaves.'

Margaret Elizabeth Sangster

WINTER

'People don't notice whether it's
winter or summer when they're happy.'

Anton Chekhov

One of the nicest
ways to feel happy
is to make someone
else happy.

Winter is the time when you have the opportunity to draw in your energy and to reflect. Days become shorter, making many want to scurry back to the warmth and comfort of their own homes. Whilst there may not be so much colour and obvious beauty to be found in winter nature, there is much to enjoy about the pared back and barer landscapes. It is the opportunity to see life in a clearer and less cluttered way; to go back to basics and to think about what matters most to you. It is a time to create cozy moments of warmth and comfort and take great joy in them.

It is important to mention that some people struggle more with winter than any other season. If this is true for you, it is especially important to find ways to combat that by nurturing yourself. If you relish the colder weather and it makes you feel alive, that is wonderful. Whatever your initial reaction to winter, there are a lot of exercises to explore in this season, so enjoy discovering what resonates with you.

Whilst having intentions for each season can be helpful and uplifting, winter could be a time when you don't have many, as the need to retreat may be strong. You might find it harder to work out what makes you happy in the colder, darker weather. Please don't worry as this section offers you plenty of suggestions to help you determine what will make you the happiest. There is a chance at the end to formulate some goals so that you can clarify what works best for you.

CONNECTION

LINK WITH YOUR WINTER HAPPINESS

Write the following heading on a large sheet of paper:

Happiness in winter is...

Without thinking too much about it or trying to force any positive thoughts to surface, jot down what this means to you. Put down as many things as you can, without censoring or judging them. They can be as large or as small as you wish. Everything is relevant and nothing is unimportant. You may notice, as you focus without pressuring yourself, that quite a few things come to mind. If very little comes at first, that is fine. You don't have to rush this exercise; you can come back to it at any time.

You may notice that what you don't like surfaces, too; if that happens frequently, try to flip those thoughts into something you like. For example, if you're thinking 'It's cold and wet', you could write down 'The cold and wet means I can enjoy more indoor treats'. Only do this if it's true for you; it is important to be honest with yourself.

Once you have finished, re-read the things you have written, notice what makes you feel the most uplifted and circle them.

This exercise will give you a good insight into your personal relationship with winter and how you feel. Now you can enjoy exploring all the suggestions that follow.

BODY

MINI BURSTS OF MOVEMENT

With the cold of winter, inertia can set in. A bit like a hibernating bear, you may have the urge to eat and then sleep more, with exercise feeling like too much of an effort. A good way to combat this is to commit to short bursts of activity, so that you don't build up a barrier to exercising – and it is easier to fit it in any time in between other daily tasks.

Your bursts of activity can be really short – even 30 seconds! March fast for half a minute, or do star jumps if you want to push yourself. The rush of endorphins from small amounts of intense energy can work wonders for circulation and this can have a positive impact on your mental state.

Why not create a list of various exercises that you can do and then enjoy doing a different one every time? It will stop boredom from setting in through repetition. The wonderful side effect of this is that a short burst of just 30 seconds often sets off a desire to do another 30 seconds of something else. Before you know it, you will have done several minutes of uplifting exercise that makes you feel good.

TOUCH

COZY UP TO THOSE YOU LOVE

Whilst some associate winter with withdrawing from others, if you have a partner, it is a wonderful time for increasing or reviving closeness. The opportunity of being together in the dark evenings means more time to cozy up with meals or moments of relaxation.

You don't have to make big or protracted efforts as even small, simple gestures can create a happy sensation of warmth and contact, especially if they are done mindfully. When you hug someone you love, especially if you're cold, commit fully to the hug, letting all your senses come into play and allowing yourself to feel their warmth.

Mindfulness can turn a casual touch into something joyous on a deep level, raising oxytocin levels, leaving you with a wonderfully warm and fuzzy feeling of completeness and connection. The juxtaposition of cold weather with a warm touch can make the sensations even sweeter.

FINGERTIP TOUCH

If you are alone, you can enjoy heightened sensations through touch as well. You can make your fingertips more sensitive by rubbing them together lightly. Try it now by brushing your index finger tips together against each other for at least 20 seconds. Then run each index finger gently down either side of your face. Isn't it amazing how much more you can feel as a result?

WONDER

ZOMBIE FIRES

A good way to appreciate the emotional effects of hot and cold in winter is to look at the extraordinary phenomenon of zombie fires.

Zombie fires are burning embers left from scorching hot summer fires that burrow under carbon-rich peat soil and remain smouldering even as they are covered by blankets of winter snow. When the snow eventually melts, the embers are still there, ready to burst into further fires.

Think about this in relation to parts of you that may feel as though they become buried in the winter: your body is swathed in thicker layers of clothes; your energy to bounce out of bed early in the morning could be diminished and walks in the late evening sunshine aren't on offer.

Yet, whatever aspects of you are curtailed by winter, they are still there underneath, simmering away, ready to emerge again in the spring. What if you learn to love sheltering parts of yourself during this time? What aspects of yourself would you like to 'put away', knowing, even as you do this, that they are alive still and simply quietly there in the background?

FIND WONDER IN WHAT IS HIDDEN

Sit or lie comfortably, close your eyes and focus on your breathing for a few moments.

Now think about the zombie fires. Visualize them if you can. They are embers from summer fires, still alive and smouldering under the surface of the earth, with the soil covered in layers of snow. It isn't an effort for them to exist; they are simply there, protected and very much alive in their cocoon. How do you feel as you imagine this?

As you relax, ask yourself what elements of you are like this in winter. Take your time. Which part of you feels the most like those embers? Why? Focus on that part of you for a moment.

The hotter zombie fires burn during the summer, the more they thrive through the winter. So, if your embers relate to something that is vibrant and energized in summer, you are mirroring nature.

Now consider the conditions in which the embers survive: the carbon-rich, peat soil and the layers of snow. Why are your embers alive? What are the ingredients that ensure they are safe rather than extinguished? What is your soil? Your snow?

How important is it to nurture all these parts of you through the winter? How do you want to do that? When do you want your snow to melt? When do you want those embers to burst forth into flames? You may find different elements of you want to emerge at different times and that is fine.

When you want to stop, imagine the zombie fires retreating in your mind's eye; see them disappearing into the distance. Take your time before you open your eyes and notice how your body feels heavy and relaxed.

This exercise can be revisited at different times and you may notice different thoughts crop up for you on each occasion.

UNDERSTANDING

LEARNING MORE ABOUT NATURE

Here is another lovely winter nature fact for you to consider and research further if you wish. Extending your knowledge of our amazing world is a great way to increase your joy.

Most people think of butterflies emerging from a chrysalis, but did you know that a few species emigrate or lie dormant in their full form through the winter? The mourning cloak (also known as the Camberwell beauty) is a wonderful example as they fold up their wings and shelter under bark for the entire winter.

This is another reminder how, like many creatures in nature, we remain 'whole' through the winter, resting as needed, ready to emerge refreshed when the time is right. Learning to relish this phase and to welcome it can add a lot of happiness to your winter.

MOVEMENT

DANCING TO THE MUSIC

Balancing rest with exercise is essential as you need to make sure your endorphins become activated in a season when often they can be neglected. For some people, it can be hard to find the motivation to exercise, so it can be helpful to 'think outside the box' for exercise during winter.

One of your winter activities could be dancing to your favourite music. Put on some uplifting dance music – the kind that makes it impossible for you to sit still. You know that feeling when you just have to tap your foot or sway and, before you know it, you are on your feet? That kind of music! Try doing something different when you dance, even something silly and fun, like touching every object in the room as you move or picking up an object and dancing with it. Anything goes, as long as you enjoy it and it's safe.

FRESH AIR

Going for a brisk walk in the cold can be refreshing, mentally as well as physically. If you feel stuck indoors or if something is on your mind, one of the great benefits of going for a walk is that the physical act of moving your body forward can help your thoughts to move forward, too. The contrast of the warmth as you come in from even a short cold walk is another happiness booster, setting off those feel-good endorphins.

MOTIVATION IS KEY

If you struggle with motivation, offer yourself a reward when you do a certain amount of exercise. It doesn't have to be a food treat; it could be playing a video game, watching a favourite episode of something that makes you feel good or soaking in an essence-scented bath – whatever you think of as a nice treat. Incentivizing yourself during winter is especially important – and fun! Work out what means the most to you so that your motivation remains high.

Lastly, if exercise is more of an effort for you during winter, think of it this way: people save money so that they can enjoy a holiday or indulge in their favourite hobby; the act of putting aside money regularly throughout the year makes that eventual joy possible. In the same way, if you commit to a small amount of exercise or meditation every day, you are investing in your long-term health and that in turn will increase your happiness levels in every way: physically, mentally, emotionally and spiritually.

SCENT

FRAGRANCE TO MAKE YOU HAPPY

Scent in your home feels especially important in the winter when you may be indoors more. Here is a simple suggestion for your bedroom so you can enjoy your time there: change your bed linen more often so you have the lovely feeling of sliding between clean fabric. Treat yourself to an essential oil that helps you relax, such as lavender or chamomile. You can put a few drops of it on a tissue and have it beside your bed or near your pillow.

During the day, if you feel the need for something uplifting, try an astringent oil to cleanse and invigorate, such as rosemary or eucalyptus. Ylang ylang is said to affect some people very positively – it has an unusual scent that can prompt a strong 'love it or hate it' response. If you haven't smelled it before, find a sample in a health shop and discover for yourself which way you react.

SMUDGING TO CLEAR THE AIR

During the winter, you can get rid of stagnant energy in your home by burning sage sticks or holy wood (palo santo) and wafting them around each room. The cold weather may mean you open your windows and doors less often, so this can be an uplifting way to clear the air, literally as well as spiritually.

SUSTAINING WINTER FOOD

Winter cooking can produce aromas that get your tastebuds going into overdrive too. Many healthy meals that are hearty and warming will waft delicious smells through your home. Food is personal so find the cooking aromas that give you most pleasure. There are so many enticing choices. Alternatively, simply peeling satsumas and enjoying their sweet taste is another delightful way to fill the room with an uplifting scent.

NURTURE

COZY INTO WINTER

Cozy is a word that crops up frequently in relation to how people can feel during winter months. When you reflect on that word, how appropriate does it feel for you in relation to this season in particular? What does the word 'cozy' mean to you?

There are some wonderful dictionary descriptions: snug, comfortable, informal, intimate, pleasant, homely, sheltered, tucked up, cuddled up, snuggled down.

What about creating an area at home that becomes a special cozy place for you during the winter? It might be an area in which you already sit, but you can adapt it and then change it as you go through the seasons.

Winter is the season with less sunshine when you have the perfect excuse to rest and build up your energy for the coming spring. Provided you are balancing yourself with some exercise for your endorphin 'fix', how wonderful to take the opportunity to relax more during this season. Take comfort from this passage by Lewis Carroll:

'I wonder if the snow loves the trees and fields that it kisses them so gently? And then it covers them up snug, you know, with a white quilt; and perhaps it says, "Go to sleep, darlings, till the summer comes again."'

CREATING A COZY SPACE

There are lovely items you could choose to have around
you during the winter, such as a velvety soft blanket in which
to snuggle. If you don't have a fireplace, you could put a
real-time fire video on your television or computer and
light scented candles, such as pine and spicy cinnamon.
Warming incense can be comforting and relaxing, too. If you
see family and friends less during this time, perhaps bring
photos of them a little closer to you. Put books you want to
read within easy reach. Ask yourself what else appeals to you
and contributes to your feeling of cozy happiness and find
space for it.

If you are affected by SAD (Seasonal Affective Disorder),
investing in a light box might be very helpful for the winter
season. Even if you sit in front of it for short periods only, it
can lift your mood.

CREATIVITY

SHARE CREATIVE PASTIMES

Why not do something fun for a loved one? There are many indoor activities, both mental and physical, that can uplift you during this season. If you have children and/or grandchildren, a scavenger or treasure hunt might be enjoyable. Of course, adults might like this too! You can link it to a theme they enjoy to increase the sense of fun. Making simple things, whether alone or with others, such as cutting out paper chains and painting them, can be a nice way to pass some time too.

Book clubs are a positive pastime, especially in the winter, but if you don't want to organize one, you could create an event where each person has to find the most uplifting piece of poetry, song or piece of art relating to winter that they can, and then share them with the group. You could all vote on the most uplifting piece and give a prize.

SPICE UP THE SEASON

If you want to raise your endorphin levels, here is an unusual suggestion you might enjoy. You may have learned already that eating some dark chocolate is an endorphin inducer (see page 27), but did you know that eating hot chilli peppers can do this too? Capsaicin is the compound that gives the 'burn' to the chilli pepper and when your body feels that heat, endorphins kick in to quench the fire. If you want a very different, creative approach to happiness levels during the winter, you could try a pepper-tasting party! It is an innovative way to keep warm during winter.

BREATHING

CLEANSE AND ENERGIZE BREATHING

Here is the first of two breathing suggestions for the winter season; this one is designed to cleanse and re-energize you. As a bonus, it will help release endorphins in your body too.

There are several variations on this breathing technique, but here is a basic and simple one that most people can do safely. As always, if you feel uncomfortable or unwell when you try it, stop and return to normal breathing. It is best to have an empty stomach when you do this; please avoid if you have had a big meal. Be seated with your feet flat on the floor and have an upright, but not stiff, posture.

Breathe in fully, through your nose if possible, and then breathe out sharply and speedily through your mouth, pulling your belly in and upwards as you do so, forcing your lungs to empty. Your next inhalation will come easily after that. If you breathe in to a count of one and exhale to a count of three, you may be able to feel as though you have emptied your lungs fully. Repeat several times, up to ten if you wish, but there is no pressure to do that many, especially initially. Stop if you feel dizzy. Let your breath return to normal before you stand up.

There are more variations if you find this kind of breathing helpful, such as breathing in and out through your nose only. You can read about the yogic *kapalabhati* breath to understand more and experiment with advanced methods.

RELAXING BREATH

This breathing exercise will help you to breathe more deeply and thus relax you, again releasing those feel-good endorphins. If you have created a cozy space for yourself, it would be lovely to try this exercise there. Sit in a relaxed but upright position with your feet flat on the floor, or lie down, with your legs stretched out if possible and your arms slightly away from your sides.

Take a few moments to focus on your breathing, without trying to alter it in any way. Just enjoy each in- and out-breath. When you feel relaxed, try breathing in to a count of two and then out to a count of four. Repeat this count several times. Then, when you feel ready, try breathing in to a count of three and out to a count of six. Repeat several times. Then try to increase with a four/eight count and so on. Only go as far as you wish. The benefit of this exercise lies in enjoying the sensations as your breath slows down, not in competing with yourself to see how far you can go. Experiment with the numbers you use but the breath out should always be a longer count than the breath in. You can also do a variation where you pause for a few seconds before each in-breath. Only do what feels good for you.

This is particularly good for releasing stress and inducing a lovely state of calm because it will activate serotonin in your body. It could become a routine part of nurturing yourself during winter.

MEDITATION

CREATING A PROTECTIVE FIELD

Sit or lie comfortably and let yourself settle. Close your eyes. Feel your body relax. Notice your breathing without altering it. When you feel comfortable, try to focus on the space your body is taking up. Where are the physical edges to each part of your body? Slowly trace your outline in your mind and become aware of where your body stops and the air surrounds you.

Now think of your body as it moves through your daily routine. How often is it in contact with outside elements, such as clothes, furniture, other objects or tools, water, cold, air and food? Reflect on how often your physical body comes into contact with something or someone else...

How protected does your body feel during the day? When might you feel vulnerable?

Now consider the energy of any other people or creatures you may find yourself in contact with during each day. How does their energy affect you? When is it uplifting and when it is draining? As you become aware of this, reflect on how important it is for you to feel protected and comfortable, whatever your interactions during the day.

Now think about what image represents protection to you. Say the word 'protect' silently to yourself and notice what happens. It may be a solid image like a cloak, a suit of armour, a wall or even a crystal. It could be a sound, smell or taste. It might a protective symbol or a creature that represents strength and protection. Whatever comes is right for you and will be personal to you.

Now ask yourself how you need that protection to manifest itself in your everyday life so that you feel safe and happy. Take your time and know that it is personal to you. No one else needs to know about it or to understand it. It might be something physical that you want or something on a spiritual, emotional or mental level that resonates powerfully for you.

When you feel comfortable with what you have created, test it out by imagining yourself in a slightly vulnerable position and then pull up your protection. How is it making you feel? If you feel good, that is wonderful. If you feel you want to create something stronger, return to this exercise when you can and keep experimenting.

When you are ready to finish, take a moment to conjure up your protection and then gently open your eyes and slowly reorient yourself to your day.

FEELING SAFE

Feeling protected and safe gives you greater freedom to explore your emotions. When you understand yourself, and accept how you are, you are more confident. This, in turn, makes it much easier to embrace happiness. That is why this meditation is powerful. Keep testing your protection and see how well it works for you. Enjoy experimenting with different types of protection until you find the most effective one for you.

REFLECTION AND INTENTION

You have been encouraged to try a lot of different ways to explore happiness during winter. Which methods have been most powerful for you? You may have a clearer sense of the intentions that will boost your happiness during winter and, if so, it would be helpful for you to make notes and decide how you want to keep the momentum going through to spring. Small, specific targets are easier to meet than one big one, so make them realistic. Check that you will enjoy the tasks before you commit to them, so that you feel motivated to complete them.

On the following pages, there are some further thoughts for you to consider.

TEACH YOURSELF TO RECEIVE GRATEFULLY

Whilst winter is a time when you may want to retreat, one of the great antidotes to feeling negative about this is to remember to factor in moments of giving and receiving with a full and grateful heart. Many people say it is easier to give than to receive so, when you consider the logic of that, if it makes you feel good to give, then you need people who are willing to receive in order for you to feel fulfilled. If you are someone who finds it hard to receive, it is helpful to realize that receiving something gratefully means you enable another person to feel good about their giving to you.

What about having an intention through winter of consciously accepting and expressing appreciation for all gifts from others – whether that be their time, a compliment or something they do for you or give to you? You could make a winter plan for how you will do this, committing to certain connections and communication.

DECLUTTER YOUR LIFE

Winter can symbolize a sense of paring back and decluttering, too. Just like the trees let go and lose their leaves, you can think about anything you want to let go of during winter months. It could involve practical tasks such as clearing out old clothes or items around the house. Equally, it could mean releasing unwanted emotional baggage. Think about what you would like to shed and then make a realistic goal. Remember that small, separate goals are more likely to be achieved than one large one.

LEARN TO LET GO

If you are struggling to discover what you want to shed, think of a symbolic image, such as a bare tree alone in a field, and ask yourself what needs to happen for you to achieve that simplicity for yourself. You might want to imagine fallen leaves around the base of the tree and assign images or words to some of them, so that you can see what you need to release in order to find that sense of peace. It may take you a while to let go of what you don't want. Humans are complicated and can cling onto things for different reasons.

What matters is having the courage to explore what will make you happier, the wisdom to know how to make it happen, and then having compassion with yourself as you find ways to let go of what doesn't nurture and support you, so you can embrace and enjoy what makes you truly happy.

Anyone who lives in harmony with themselves lives in harmony with the universe.

WINTER AFFIRMATIONS

Winter is a time to reflect as you enjoy retreating from colder weather. Let yourself rest and embrace the welcome feeling of renewal that ensues.

'Relaxation is good for my soul.'

'I nurture myself every day.'

'I enjoy resting my body.'

'Every day I renew myself.'

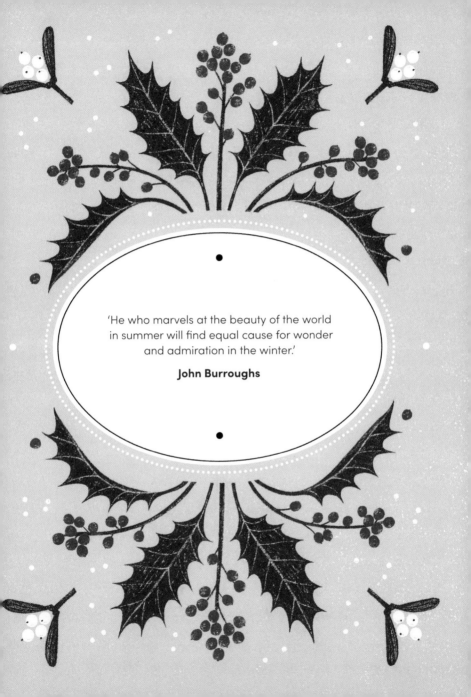

'He who marvels at the beauty of the world in summer will find equal cause for wonder and admiration in the winter.'

John Burroughs

ABOUT THE AUTHOR

Tara Ward is a best-selling author on personal development and spiritual wellbeing with sales of more than half a million copies worldwide. She has worked in more than 40 countries across five continents developing new ways to improve communication between all cultures: physically, mentally, emotionally and spiritually. Tara has published 14 books including *Mindful Journaling*, *The Healing Handbook: A Spiritual Guide to Healing Yourself and Others*, *Discover Meditation & Mindfulness* and *The Book of Healing*. She also runs workshops and gives talks on meditation and mindfulness.

ACKNOWLEDGEMENTS

I am deeply grateful for the love and support I have from my three families: Ward, Lonnen and Rakitzis! Thank you.

I also want to thank my literary agent, Fiona Lindsay at Limelight Management, who is my unwavering support, as well as being a fount of knowledge, and the fantastic team at Quadrille, including Sarah Lavelle, Stacey Cleworth and Katherine Keeble. Thank you, too, to Anastasia Stefurak for her beautiful artwork, and for the hard work of editor, Wendy Hobson. Writing a good book is the first challenge, but having a great team to put it all together is equally important, and I am blessed with Quadrille. Thank you.

MANAGING DIRECTOR
Sarah Lavelle

ILLUSTRATOR
Anastasia Stefurak

COMMISSIONING EDITOR
Stacey Cleworth

HEAD OF PRODUCTION
Stephen Lang

SENIOR DESIGNER
Katherine Keeble

PRODUCTION CONTROLLER
Lisa Fiske

Published in 2022 by Quadrille,
an imprint of Hardie Grant Publishing

Quadrille
52–54 Southwark Street
London SE1 1UN
quadrille.com

Cataloguing in Publication Data: a catalogue record for this book
is available from the British Library.

ISBN 978 1 78713 887 2

Printed in China

FINAL AFFIRMATIONS

Repeat these affirmations frequently each day.
It will encourage and reinforce your happiness
throughout the year.

'Each season brings me joy.'

'My soul is filled with happiness.'

'I choose happiness.'

'I am happy with what I have right now.'